HOME SERIES

HOME SERIES
CLASSIC HOMES

BETA-PLUS

CONTENTS

8   Foreword

12   The redesign of an exclusive dream house
28   A warm home
42   A modern design for a historic farmhouse
48   A contemporary country house
56   Authentic and timeless
68   Simplicity and luxury in a timeless apartment
78   A duplex with wonderful proportions
96   Minimalism in a cosy setting
104   A contemporary facelift for a classic home
110   A symbiosis of elegance and functionality

P. 4-5
A project by 'Aksent. A Wanda
sofa and a Valentino chaise
longue in blue mohair. A coffee
table in morado wood and
bronze.

P. 6
A project by Frank Tack:
custom-built craftsmanship.

FOREWORD

Classic living is not bound by fleeting trends: it is the expression of good taste and sophistication. It is a style that stands the test of time without ever looking dated.
The credo: upholding fixed, traditional values such as the beauty of durable natural materials, craftsmanship, authenticity and the quality of life. It's all about harmony, aesthetics and a subtle balance.

The secret of a classic and timeless interior is often based on the ingenious combination of various elements in a way that avoids a dull and lifeless "total look". This approach goes against the movement within contemporary decorative styles that aims to anchor interiors within short periods of time and passing fashions. The designers of timeless interiors reveal their mastery in the subtle and harmonious combination of creative ideas, colours and materials.
Simple design with imaginative touches, a mixture of antique pieces, in classic or exotic styles, and beautiful designer furniture and objects: these are the ingredients of a classic and timeless interior.

This book presents ten very different interiors that all have one thing in common: each of them conveys an atmosphere of timeless elegance.

P. 8
Warm, white painted panelling for this corner of a country house. The railway door handles are from the Lerou collection.

P. 10-11
A project by Alexander Cambron and Fabienne Dupont.

THE REDESIGN

OF AN EXCLUSIVE DREAM HOUSE

F ollowing a successful business career, Alexander Cambron became an estate agent specialising in turn-key dream homes.

Alexander Cambron, a dynamic forty-something, now creates around three ready-to-use residential top-quality projects every year: "pret-à-habiter" homes, with the focus entirely on the wishes and requirements of the new owners.

The exclusive country home in this report, originally designed by Vlassak-Verhulst, is a perfect illustration of this philosophy and way of working. The interior was created by Fabienne Dupont.

The modern look of the interior contrasts with the classic outer appearance of the house. The impressive entrance hall occupies the full height of the building.

The home office has a calm atmosphere, with a view of the surrounding greenery. On the other side of the see-through fireplace are the home cinema and the second sitting room.
The living and working areas are connected, but doors can be used to separate them if required.

P. 16-17
A parquet floor in bleached oak (30cm planks) in this space between the sitting room and the office.

In the kitchen, Fabienne Dupont has combined dark oak veneer with splashes of bright red.

P. 20-21
The health and relaxation space, with a gym, hammam, jacuzzi and a swimming pool with a floor that can be raised to turn the space into a reception area. The large sliding doors open onto the sun deck and fill this space with light.

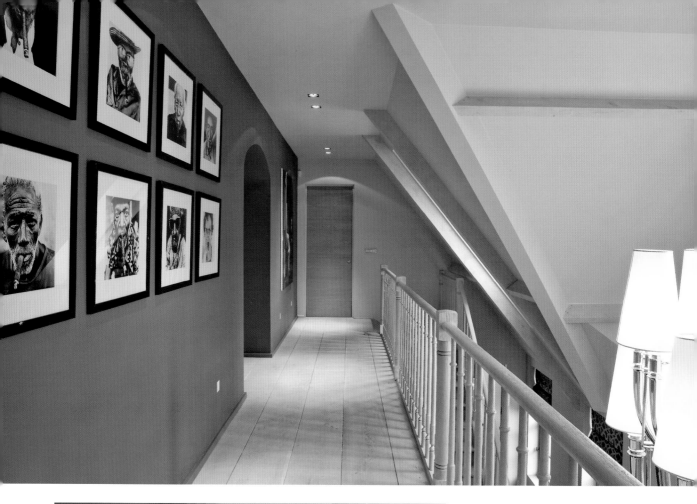

This long, open corridor leads to the bedrooms and looks out over the entrance hall.

The master bedroom in black and white with an open fireplace connecting the dressing room and bedroom. All of the rooms have a view of the back garden.

The black dressing room of the
master suite is in oak veneer,
with a see-through gas fire.

A WARM HOME

This report features one of Mi Casa's most recent projects: the perfect example of a classic, stylish home where the focus is on quality of life and a cosy, enjoyable living environment.

Solid wood houses make stylish, cosy and timeless homes.

Mi Casa uses the time-honoured technique of the dovetail joint in the construction of its homes. They pile solid wooden beams on top of one another, connecting them with a tongue and groove method and securing them at each corner. This approach means that there are no crossing beams, so the interior walls are not interrupted, and the cavity insulation can extend through the exterior walls.

The interior walls are made of solid wood beams in Norway red pine and the exterior is in brick or cedar wood, depending on local construction regulations.

Some of the major advantages of wood construction are the architectural freedom, the dry construction method and the speed of completion.

Mi Casa strives to create beautiful, personalised homes, in which the architecture and decoration reflect the philosophy and wishes of the owners. The wood of the Norway red pine exhibits more natural warmth and charm than the wood of local trees.

Their natural appearance means that wooden walls require little decoration. The owner immediately feels at home because the walls do not seem bare and unfinished or cause the room to echo unpleasantly.

A MODERN DESIGN

FOR A HISTORIC FARMHOUSE

The Cretenburghoeve is a listed building dating back to the eighteenth century (1771). The building had fallen into disrepair and urgent restoration was needed to prevent collapse.

Pas-partoe interiors did all of the work inside the farmhouse, while architect K. Beeck, a specialist in the restoration of historic buildings, coordinated the exterior work. Ballmore landscaped the garden.

Pas-partoe created a bright, open home, which has a simple appearance, yet uses classic, high-quality materials.
The company created clean views through the building by concealing any elements, such as radiators, that might disturb the lines.

The restoration work took two years. Some sections of the building had to be carefully dismantled and then painstakingly rebuilt, including walls, roof trusses, floors and the roof itself.

The result: a distinctive historic farmhouse has been beautifully restored to its former glory.

Chair supplied by pas-partoe.
The red one-seater is an LCW chair by Eames.
The table in the sitting room is a Piet Boon design.

Sandblasted oak is combined with
smooth bluestone in the kitchen. A
large sliding panel conceals the
kitchen appliances. The custom-made
table is based on a design by pas-
partoe.
The organic form of the "Tulip" chairs
by Eero Saarinen contrasts with the
straight lines of the fitted kitchen
units and table.

The parents' bedroom, also with an Orizzonti bed.
A simply designed standing lamp from Pas-partoe.

Exposed roof beams in the attic.

Shower in marble mosaic with Vola taps.
Indirect light behind the mirrors.

A CONTEMPORARY

COUNTRY HOUSE

T his completely customised country house is a total-concept project by architect Annik Dierckx and can be adapted to suit different stages of life, from a young working family to a retired couple with reduced mobility.

The architect designed every detail of the architecture and the interior, so that all of the elements are perfectly attuned, creating a home with an atmosphere of harmony and serenity.
Classic elements have been combined with modern design throughout this house.

A double oak door leads from the entrance hall into the living room. A perpendicular axis runs from the front door to the sitting room, all the way through to the open fireplace. Fire is an important element in the living areas.

The living room runs through into the
dining room and the television room.
The television room has a gas fireplace.
From the dining table, you can see the
fire in the television room, because all
of the rooms are connected.
The large sliding doors in the oak wall
can separate the television room from
the sitting and dining room if required.

The parents' bedroom is reached via the dressing room, which also provides access to the main bathroom and the library. A sliding panel creates a connection between the bedroom and bathroom. The witty antique chandelier contrasts with the plain, dark-tinted oak units in the dressing room and bedroom.

The furniture in the guest room is in wengé. The tropical wood lends warmth to this space and to the adjoining bathroom.

The main bathroom, like the rest of the house, is completely accessible for wheelchairs. Dark-tinted oak has been used here too, for the bath surround and washbasin units. Sand on the beach was the inspiration for the bathroom floor. The textured sand-coloured ceramic tiles have a natural anti-slip finish.

AUTHENTIC AND TIMELESS

Doran for Country Cooking designs and creates its own individual range of interior architecture for construction and renovation projects.

A team of interior architects and colour consultants works together to develop complete customised interiors.

These home concepts are always designed with a touch of timelessness and with a harmonious combination of forms and colours. Every element of the design concept is a unique piece.

Doran for Country Cooking builds complete interiors in contemporary and rustic styles, using the kitchen and dining area as a starting point. Traditional craftsmanship is the theme running through all of the company's projects.

An old-fashioned tap
with a solid stone
washbasin. Wooden
unit by Doran.

The rustic-style linen room, with units in painted wood and a bluestone surface. Stone tiles on the floor from the "fleur de lys" collection.

P. 59-63
A country kitchen with a cast-iron
Nobel stove and oak units with
bluestone surfaces. The traditionally
produced wall tiles are part of the
Doran collection.

The bathroom is equipped with a walk-in shower, fitted pine units and an oak door from the Doran collection.

The dressing-room cupboards are in painted MDF with an oak surface.

A bleached oak floor from the Doran collection.
Pine wall unit with an oak surface and a built-in linen cupboard.

SIMPLICITY AND LUXURY

IN A TIMELESS APARTMENT

Costermans Villaprojecten created this timeless luxury apartment in collaboration with Jan des Bouvrie's Studio Het Arsenaal. They designed a powerful concept behind the classic Parisian-style façade, with key features including high ceilings, lots of light, and rooms that are spacious, yet cosy.

Natural shades and materials were used, combined with flashes of purple and lilac.

Art from the Arsenaal collection provides the finishing touch.

The living room has a cosy sitting area in front of the simple gas fire.
A streamlined design for the bookshelves behind the armchairs.

P. 70-71
The cheerful cushions in muted shades lend a warm, playful touch to the sitting room. The lamps are by Verner Panton.

The kitchen/dining room has a table made from reclaimed pallet wood. Handle-free doors in a glossy white finish, with a Corian surface.

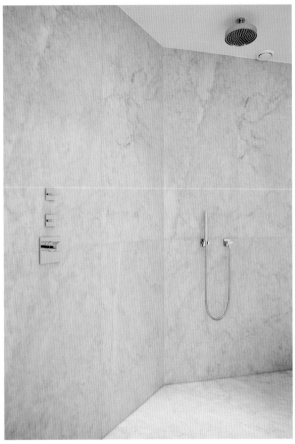

A harmony of Carrara marble and oak floorboards.
The oak floor runs throughout the apartment, creating a sense of space and continuity.

A romantic bedroom with a compact desk.

A DUPLEX

WITH WONDERFUL PROPORTIONS

T his duplex penthouse on the Belgian coast is unusual in many respects. This is a very large apartment with both the charm and floor space (over 1000m^2) of a country house, but with a unique sea view.

The home has been finished to a very high standard throughout. Obumex designed and created the ground floor, while interior architect Philip Simoen was responsible for the design of the upstairs rooms, which were also created by Obumex.

The entrance hall with its Cotto d'Este floor in flamed Buxy.
Curtains by Sahco Hesslein.

P. 80-83
The sitting area with its sea view. Furniture
from the JNL Collection. Upholstery and
curtains by Sahco Hesslein.

P. 84-87
Fireplace and TV corner designed and built by Obumex.
JNL seats with fabric by Sahco Hesslein.

JNL furniture was also selected for the dining room.

The master bedroom and dressing room, designed and created by Obumex. JNL bedroom furniture with Sahco Hesslein fabrics.

The hallway and stairs to the
guestrooms. Lighting by Stéphane
Davidts.

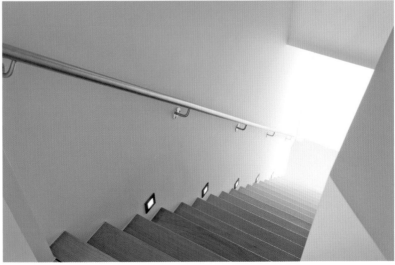

A guestroom with soft
furnishings by Sahco Hesslein.

MINIMALISM IN A COSY SETTING

F rancis Luypaert is a renowned interior architect with a prefe-rence for simple, streamlined designs within a warm and cosy atmosphere.

This report features some of his recent projects.

Francis Luypaert was commissioned to carry out a complete renovation of this entrance hall, in a streamlined contemporary style with an atmosphere of class and elegance.

The fitted furniture is in a combination of oak veneer, some of which reflects the colour of the walls, with the rest in a dark shade.

Floor in unveined Pietra Piasentina with a flamed finish. Window with a concealed frame.

The upstairs corridor with fitted cupboards painted to match the walls in a matte white. This colour is combined with a solid oak parquet in a straight grain, which has been treated with an oil-varnish finish.
The chaise longue is upholstered with a cotton fabric.

Clients are welcomed in this space in Francis Luypaert's showroom, which features an elaborate design in neutral white surroundings. The table (in MDF with a high-gloss finish) is a Luypaert design with retro-style 1970s chairs, renovated with matte white leather.
Chrome modular lighting (Bolster) and white half-pipe.
A ceramic statue by Lieven Demunter and a painting by Francis Luypaert. On the floor, a zebra-skin rug.

The children's bathroom is in shades of greige.
Bathroom furniture in hand-painted MDF.
The shower and the wall behind the washbasin are tiled with zelliges.
Surface in polished Moleanos stone. Wall lights by Stéphane Davidts.

The spacious master bathroom has a bath, walk-in shower and practical, fitted storage cupboards with classic wood panelling. A "rain shower" is built into the ceiling.
The shower walls are in tumbled marble mosaic.
The surrounds of the washbasin and bath are in polished Emperador Dark with a classic edge design.

A CONTEMPORARY FACELIFT

FOR A CLASSIC HOME

I nterior architect Stephanie Laporte (The Office Belgium) was commissioned to give a facelift to this elegant home in Ieper (Ypres).

This grand house underwent a complete metamorphosis, with its classic architecture giving way to a minimalist and streamlined contemporary look.

Stephanie Laporte also designed everything in the bar. Wall units in dark wood, combined with a mirror and lacquered glass. A light with a cascade of crystal chains.

P. 106-107
A view from the sitting
room into the dining room.

A SYMBIOSIS OF ELEGANCE

AND FUNCTIONALITY

Bourgondisch Kruis offers one of the most extensive collections of Burgundy slabs and natural stone, which can be used for floors, stairs, fireplaces, columns, and many other purposes.

The team from Bourgondisch Kruis uses these historic construction materials in a wide range of restoration projects. The company also has its own carpentry workshop, where experienced professionals create perfect custom-built work based on oak panels, and a stone workshop, where Burgundy limestone and bluestone are turned into kitchen work surfaces, exclusive floors and walls, solid sinks and other attractive features for the home.

The clients can supply their own plans or receive assistance from the Bourgondisch Kruis design team.

Every project by Bourgondisch Kruis radiates an atmosphere of class, functionality and timeless style. The projects in this report are excellent examples of the company's approach.

An original Louis XIV fireplace in Burgundy stone.

A 17th-century oak floor and a three-part folding door in old oak.
Floor in old Burgundy slabs, laid in a random Roman bond. Stairs in solid Burgundy stone with a wrought-iron rail. A solid washbasin and old oak panelling.

P. 112-115
Bourgondisch Kruis designed and
created this kitchen.
Bluestone (for work surfaces,
washbasin, supports and the wall
behind the stove) is combined with
units in old oak. Floors in old bluestone
tiles (50 x 50cm).
The barbecue is in terracotta tiles with
a bluestone surround.

Wrought-iron railing and door.

A bathroom with solid washbasins in Burgundy stone with Burgundy stone slabs in a smooth finish for the floor too.

A bedroom with old oak panelling.

P. 118-119
Wardrobes with oak doors.

HOME SERIES

Volume 3 : CLASSIC HOMES

The reports in this book are selected from the Beta-Plus collection of home-design books: www.betaplus.com
They have been compiled in a special series by Le Figaro in French language: Ma Déco

Copyright © 2009 Beta-Plus Publishing / Le Figaro
Originally published in French language

PUBLISHER
Beta-Plus Publishing
Termuninck 3
B – 7850 Enghien
Belgium
www.betaplus.com
info@betaplus.com

PHOTOGRAPHY
Jo Pauwels

DESIGN
Polydem - Nathalie Binart

TRANSLATIONS
Laura Watkinson

ISBN : 9789089440341

Printed in China

P. 122-123
A streamlined contemporary kitchen designed by interior architect Filip Van Bever. Basaltina lava stone has been used throughout this project, for the floors, work surfaces and walls. Stone by Van Den Weghe.

P. 124-125
The kitchen of a farmhouse restored by Virginie and Odile Dejaegere. The aged bluestone (tiles, work surfaces, sinks) is combined with reclaimed terracotta tommettes.

P. 126-127
A project by architect Stéphane Boens. Floors in old terracotta tiles, work surfaces in red marble.